D1712292

31 DAYS TO INCREASE YOUR STRESS

BY TRICIA SEYMOUR

BLUE SKY

MARKETING INC.

BLUE SKY MARKETING INC.
PO Box 21583-S St. Paul, MN 55121 USA

31 Days to Increase Your Stress
Copyright © 1997 by Tricia Seymour
Design by Scott Drude
Tricia's Caricature by Cathy Hall, Scribbles Art Service
Edited by Vic Spadaccini
Printed in the United States of America
ISBN: 0-911493-19-0

All rights reserved. No part of this book may be reproduced or transmitted in any form or by any means, electronic or mechanical, including photocopying, recording, or by any information storage and retrieval system without written permission from the author, except for the inclusion of brief quotations in a review.

Published by:
BLUE SKY MARKETING INC.
PO Box 21583-S
St. Paul, MN 55121 USA
(612) 456-5602
(612) 456-0608 fax
SAN 263-9394
8   7   6   5   4   3   2   1

ACKNOWLEDGMENTS:

Thanks to Mom & Dad: George and Florence Seymour
Thanks to Sister Jeannette and Family: John, Bobby, Mathew, & Timothy
Thanks to Sister Kathy and Family: Michael, Michelle, & Kimberley
Thanks to Brother Georgie's Family: Brian, Kevin, & Diane
Thanks to Reverend Rusty - A gift from God!
Thanks to Gerri Slabaugh, Susan Schreifels, and Vic Spadaccini
Thanks to Friends Everywhere!!!

Thanks to the World - for buying my books!!!
Thanks to the Universe for teaching me about Stress!

Because this book was such a huge project (Ha! Ha!), I'm not even going to try to name everyone who inspired me. I know I would probably leave out a few thousand names of some very important people (or beings) who helped me along the way. I apologize for the oversight and promise to feel guilty for the rest of my earthly life (hmmm... could that be another book?). So from the bottom of my codependent heart, I thank all of you.

INTRODUCTION

Enjoy! This book is written "Tongue in Cheek" or "Foot in Mouth." Either way, it's all in good sarcastic fun!

If you see anything in this book that seems familiar—anything that you are presently doing that causes you stress—as a psychotherapist, I recommend that you STOP doing what you are doing and try something different!

If you *like* stress and *really* want to INCREASE YOUR STRESS, then practice everything in this book more than once—but don't blame me when you have a heart attack!!!

Again, Enjoy! Laughter is good medicine! I know you'll have as much fun reading this as I did writing it.

Laugh, Love, and Live Long!!!

Tricia

DAY 1
WORRY...

ESPECIALLY ABOUT THINGS YOU HAVE NO CONTROL OVER.

THINK ABOUT ALL THE TERRIBLE, AWFUL THINGS THAT COULD POSSIBLY HAPPEN TO YOU OR ANYONE YOU KNOW– SOMEDAY!

WORRYING MAKES EVERYTHING BETTER, DOESN'T IT?

DAY 2
DON'T RELAX!

PUSH PUSH PUSH, BOTH YOURSELF AND OTHERS.

T IMES A WASTIN' AND YOU MUST _ALWAYS_ BE DOING SOMETHING CONSTRUCTIVE!

DON'T REST UNTIL YOU GET IT _ALL_ DONE.

DAY 3
PROCRASTINATE

PUT OFF 'TIL TOMORROW WHAT YOU DON'T ABSOLUTELY HAVE TO DO TODAY.

WHY HURRY?

YOU DO BETTER UNDER PRESSURE.

DAY 4

AVOID DRINKING WATER AND EXERCISING

THERE'S TOO MUCH HYPE ABOUT THIS "HEALTH THING."

BESIDES,

YOU CAN ALWAYS DO SOMETHING ABOUT YOUR HEALTH _NEXT YEAR!_

DAY 5
DON'T PLAN ANYTHING

ALWAYS "WING IT."

IT'S MORE CHALLENGING THAT WAY.

GETS THE ADRENALINE GOING!

DAY 6
SLEEP LESS

YOU HAVE TOO MUCH TO DO TO SLEEP.

KEEP PUSHING YOURSELF.

DON'T BE LAZY!

DAY 7
HOLD IN EMOTIONS

OTHERS WON'T LIKE YOU IF YOU TELL THEM HOW YOU REALLY FEEL.

BETTER YET,

DON'T EVEN KNOW HOW _YOU_ FEEL!

DAY 8

ENJOY MORE COFFEE, SMOKES, AND BOOZE

YOU ONLY LIVE ONCE-

MIGHT AS WELL...

MAKE IT SHORT!

DAY 9
IGNORE YOUR OWN NEEDS

ONLY SELFISH PEOPLE CARE ABOUT THEMSELVES

AND BESIDES,

OTHERS _ARE_ MORE IMPORTANT THAN YOU.

DAY 10
LIVE UP TO EVERYONE'S EXPECTATIONS

INCLUDING,
BUT NOT LIMITED TO,
YOUR MOM,
DAD,
PARTNER,
IN-LAWS,
KIDS,
BOSS,
FRIENDS,
NEIGHBORS, CAT,
AND DOG.

DAY 11

$PEND MORE MONEY
MONEY
THAN YOU MAKE

CHARGE UP YOUR CREDIT CARDS TO THEIR LIMITS.

BORROW MORE MONEY THAN YOU COULD EVER PAY BACK;

WHO KNOWS, YOU MIGHT REALLY WIN THE LOTTERY THIS TIME!

DAY 12
DO IT ALL YOURSELF

IF YOU WANT SOMETHING DONE RIGHT-

YOU'VE GOT TO DO IT

YOURSELF!

DAY 13
BE INFLEXIBLE

DON'T GIVE IN,

MOVE, BUDGE, CHANGE, OR COMPROMISE;

IT'S A SIGN OF WEAKNESS.

DAY 14

LIFE IS FOR WORK, NOT FUN!

IF YOU'RE HAVING FUN,

YOU'RE NOT BEING PRODUCTIVE.

GET TO WORK!

DAY 15
DON'T SOCIALIZE- HIBERNATE!

CUT YOURSELF OFF FROM OTHERS.

IF YOU DO SOCIALIZE, SURROUND YOURSELF WITH NEGATIVE PEOPLE,

BECAUSE MISERY LOVES COMPANY.

DAY 16
HOLD YOUR BREATH

WHATEVER YOU DO, *DON'T* BREATHE.

YOU MIGHT LOSE CONTROL OR EVEN WORSE –

EXPERIENCE LIFE!

DAY 17
SAY "YES" TO EVERYONE ALL THE TIME

**SOMEONE MIGHT NOT LIKE YOU
IF YOU SAY "NO",**

AND IT'S _SO_ IMPORTANT THAT
EVERYONE IN THE WORLD
APPROVES OF YOU.

DON'T BLOW IT!

DAY 18
CONVINCE YOURSELF THAT CHOCOLATE IS THE "5TH" FOOD GROUP

FAT, SUGAR, AND CAFFEINE ALL IN ONE PACKAGE.

WHAT MORE

COULD A BODY ASK FOR?

DAY 19
LOSE YOUR SENSE OF HUMOR

DAY 20
BLAME OTHERS

DON'T TAKE RESPONSIBILITY FOR ANY PART OF YOUR LIFE IF YOU DON'T HAVE TO.

AFTER ALL, YOU NEVER MAKE ANY OF YOUR OWN DECISIONS,

DO YOU?

DAY 21
ALWAYS LOOK FOR WHAT'S WRONG!

CONSTANTLY LISTEN TO, READ, AND WATCH NEGATIVE THINGS.

REMIND YOURSELF

THAT IT WILL _NEVER_ GET BETTER.

DAY 22
HOLD GRUDGES...
FOREVER!

DON'T FORGIVE,

BECAUSE IT LETS "THEM" OFF THE HOOK.

DAY 23
FEEL GUILTY

YOU *SHOULD* FEEL GUILTY,

EVEN IF

YOU DON'T KNOW WHY.

DAY 24

STAY UNORGANIZED!

IT'S MORE FUN TO HUNT AROUND EVERY TIME YOU NEED SOMETHING.

BESIDES,

YOU HAVE TO HAVE A *LITTLE* EXCITEMENT IN YOUR LIFE.

DAY 25
EXPECT OTHERS TO READ YOUR MIND

AFTER ALL, IF THEY CARED ENOUGH ABOUT YOU, THEY'D BE ABLE TO,

AND BESIDES,

YOU _CAN_ READ THEIRS, CAN'T YOU?

DAY 26
BE LATE FOR EVERYTHING

MAKE THEM WAIT.

MAKE THEM THINK

YOU'RE REALLY IMPORTANT.

DAY 27
IGNORE YOUR DOCTOR'S ADVICE

IT'S TOO MUCH TROUBLE!

YOU KNOW MORE

THAN THEY DO ANYWAY!

DAY 28
TAKE THINGS PERSONALLY

THEY ARE PROBABLY

MEANT THAT WAY

ANYWAY.

DAY 29

HATE YOUR JOB

WORK ONLY BECAUSE YOU "HAVE TO" AND DON'T TRY TO CHANGE.

BESIDES,

IF YOU DID WHAT YOU LIKED, YOU'D HAVE NOTHING TO COMPLAIN ABOUT.

DAY 30
EXPECT PERFECTION FROM YOURSELF

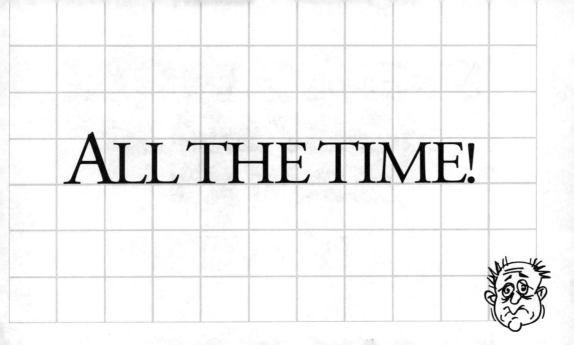

ALL THE TIME!

DAY 31

EXPECT PERFECTION FROM OTHERS

ALL THE TIME!

YOU'RE PERFECT,

WHY AREN'T THEY?

PLEASE SEND ME YOUR COMMENTS AND SUGGESTIONS!

I am planning to publish new books as often as possible (I need the money!) There will be special volumes for parents, teens, kids, salespeople, businesses, pets, couples, siblings, holidays, etc. Send me your Great Ideas (because I know I'll eventually run out of ideas myself).

Please send your comments and suggestions to me care of my publisher:

Tricia Seymour
Blue Sky Marketing Inc.
PO Box 21583
St. Paul, MN 55121 USA

Publishers Note: all items submitted become the property of the publisher and/or Tricia Seymour and there will be no compensation and we cannot guarantee credit.

PRESENTATIONS, SEMINARS, KEYNOTES

Whether you are looking for a humorous keynote address, an exciting half-day seminar, or an entertaining and educational full-day program, International Motivational Humorist Tricia Seymour is the *right* choice! She is famous for her "tongue-in-cheek" keynote "31 Days To A Miserable Life!"

She is the Perfect Person to present at your next:

Convention Kick-off or Wrap-up	Awards Program
Employee Rally	Annual Meeting
Staff Training	Conference Workshop
Or any other time you need "Edu-tainment"	

Her audiences are composed of men and women interested in personal growth and self-improvement. She has worked with people throughout the: United States, Norway, Belgium, England, Scotland, Australia, Southeast Asia.

For more information contact:
Karlsen & Seymour International
PO Box 211116 Bedford, TX 76095-8116 USA
Phone: (817) 540-2129

ABOUT THE AUTHOR

Tricia Seymour was once told she wouldn't make it. Now a successful Psycotherapist, Author, Entrepreneur, and Corporate Trainer in international demand, she has proven "them" wrong, using her talent to turn problems into opportunities.

At a young age, Tricia learned the value of humor and how not to take herself (or anyone else) too seriously. She now uses that keen sense of humor to debunk the artificially imposed limits of our everyday lives, helping others realize that they, too, can be whatever they want to be!

As a popular *"International Motivational Humorist,"* Tricia's charismatic personality is infectious. As a professional guest on TV talk shows, she has used her humor and intellect to help others deal with life. She touches hearts through humor and transforms lives.

Tricia Seymour has a Masters degree in Marriage and Family Therapy and is presently based out of Dallas, Texas.

THE 31 DAYS TO A MISERABLE LIFE SERIES

Coming Soon to a Bookstore or Merchant Near You!

31 Days to Increase Your Stress
31 Days to Ruin Your Relationship
31 Days to Lose Your Customers

31 Days to Decrease Your Wealth
31 Days to Mismanage Your Time
31 Days to Spoil Your Kids (Raising A Brat)

6 Months to a Miserable Life (6 Pack of Books, Includes all the above titles)
Miserable Life Journal
12 Month Calendar to a Miserable Life

Contact Blue Sky Marketing for a list of bookstores or merchants near you who carry these
whimsical, captivating books!

800/444-5450 OR (612) 456-5602
OR FAX (612) 456-0608